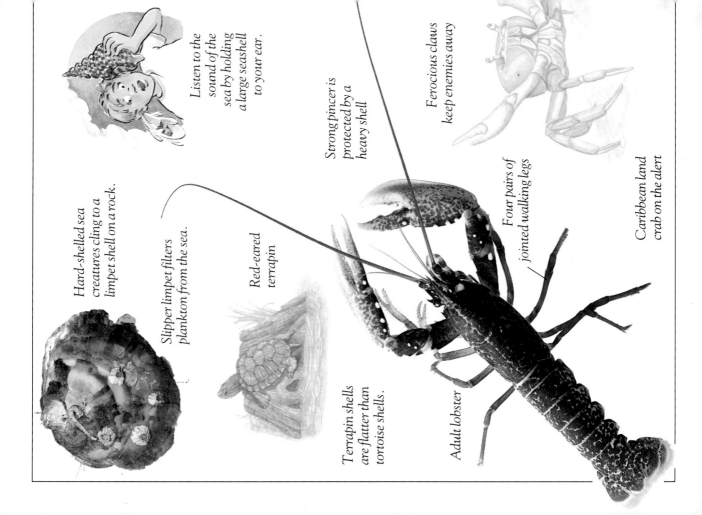

Listen to the sound of the sea by holding a large seashell to your ear.

Ferocious claws keep enemies away

Strong pincer is protected by a heavy shell

Hard-shelled sea creatures cling to a limpet shell on a rock.

Slipper limpet filters plankton from the sea.

Red-eared terrapin

Four pairs of jointed walking legs

Caribbean land crab on the alert

Terrapin shells are flatter than tortoise shells.

Adult lobster

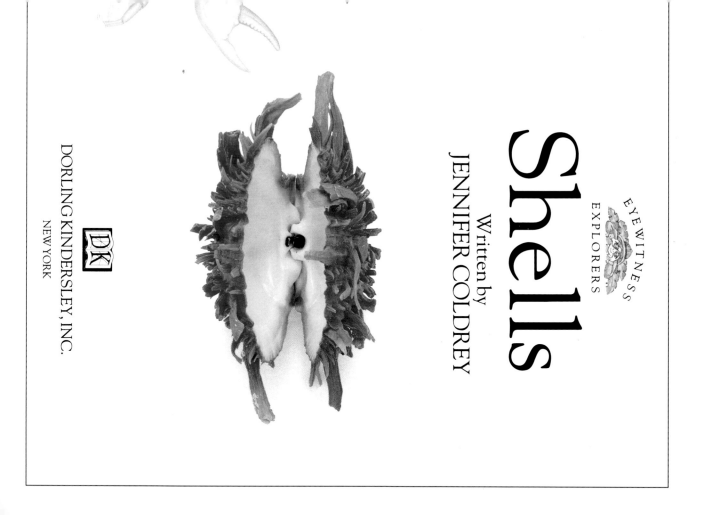

EYEWITNESS
EXPLORERS

Shells

Written by
JENNIFER COLDREY

DORLING KINDERSLEY, INC.

NEW YORK

A DORLING KINDERSLEY BOOK

Senior editor Susan McKeever   **Art editors** Thomas Keenes, Chris Legee
Assistant editor Djinn von Noorden   **U.S. editor** Charles A. Wills
Production Catherine Semark   **Editorial consultant** Kathie Way

First American Edition, 1993
2 4 6 8 10 9 7 5 3 1
Published in the United States by
Dorling Kindersley, Inc., 232 Madison Avenue
New York, New York 10016

Library of Congress Catalog Card Number 92-54311

ISBN 1-56458-229-9

Color reproduction by Colourscan, Singapore
Printed in Italy by A. Mondadori Editore, Verona

Contents

Looking at shells

Woodlands, parks, seashores, rivers, mountains – almost any habitat you can think of is home to some kind of shell. Look closely and you won't be disappointed. You can look at snails, limpets, crabs, tortoises, scallops, and more. If the shells are empty you can take them home.

Explore the shore

Look along the shoreline for crab cases and empty seashells. At low tide, search among the rocks and seaweed and in tidal pools for living shelled animals. Take a net, some plastic tubs, and a bucket for collecting shelled creatures to watch more closely.

Always put animals back where you found them.

Scallop shell

Look closely at the details of the shells you find. You can recognize a scallop shell by its fan shape and the two "ears" along the hinge of the shell.

Smooth, white inner surface

Ear of shell

Scalloped (wavy) edge of shell

Brown speckled ribs on outside of shell

Explorer's notepad

Carry a notebook and pencils with you when you look for shells. Then you can do a drawing and make some notes of what you find. Note the shape, size, and color of your shell. You may need to make several drawings to show the different parts clearly.

Note the date and place your shell was found

Night life

The best time to see snails in action is at night. Choose a warm, damp evening and go outside with a flashlight after dark. Search on paths, flowerbeds, and even up walls. Watch the snails gliding along.

Always tell an adult if you go out at night.

Tracking snails

Find some snails in their daytime hiding place. This may be under a pile of logs, a hole in a wall, or inside an old plant pot. Mark some of the snail shells with a blob of nail polish or paint. Make sure each shell has a different mark.

1 Go out with a flashlight after dark to see what happens. Have all your snails come out to feed? Follow their slimy trails to discover where they go.

2 The next day, go back to the snails' hiding place to see how many are there. Did all your snails return home after their night out?

9

What is a shell?

What do snails, oysters, crabs, and turtles have in common? They all have a shell – a hard, outer case that covers and protects a softer creature inside. A shell helps protect an animal from hungry predators. It is also a safe shelter from severe or harmful weather.

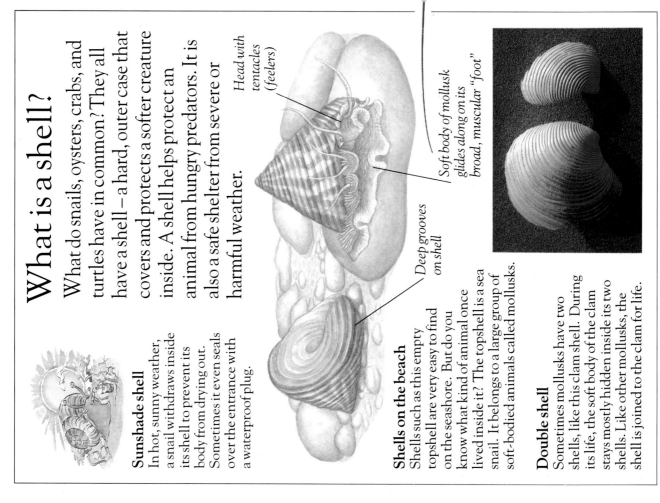

Head with tentacles (feelers)

Soft body of mollusk glides along on its broad, muscular "foot"

Deep grooves on shell

Sunshade shell

In hot, sunny weather, a snail withdraws inside its shell to prevent its body from drying out. Sometimes it even seals over the entrance with a waterproof plug.

Shells on the beach

Shells such as this empty topshell are very easy to find on the seashore. But do you know what kind of animal once lived inside it? The topshell is a sea snail. It belongs to a large group of soft-bodied animals called mollusks.

Double shell

Sometimes mollusks have two shells, like this clam shell. During its life, the soft body of the clam stays mostly hidden inside its two shells. Like other mollusks, the shell is joined to the clam for life.

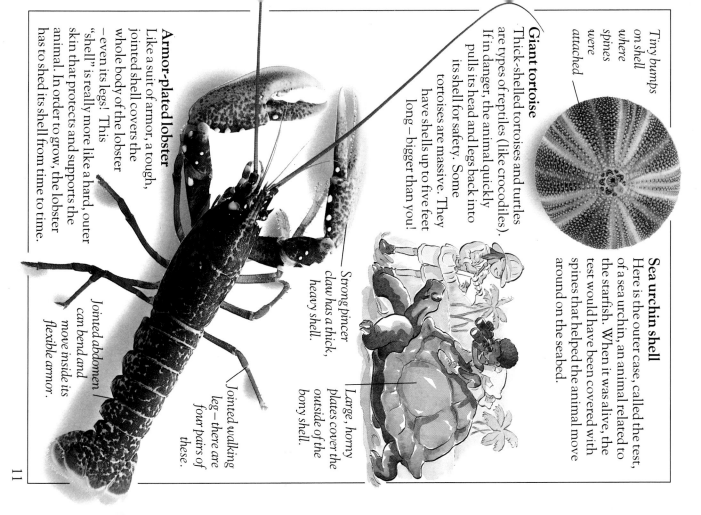

Tiny bumps on shell where spines were attached

Sea urchin shell

Here is the outer case, called the test, of a sea urchin, an animal related to the starfish. When it was alive, the test would have been covered with spines that helped the animal move around on the seabed.

Giant tortoise

Thick-shelled tortoises and turtles are types of reptiles (like crocodiles). If in danger, the animal quickly pulls its head and legs back into its shell for safety. Some tortoises are massive. They have shells up to five feet long – bigger than you!

Strong pincer claw has a thick, heavy shell.

Large, horny plates cover the outside of the bony shell.

Armor-plated lobster

Like a suit of armor, a tough, jointed shell covers the whole body of the lobster – even its legs! This "shell" is really more like a hard, outer skin that protects and supports the animal. In order to grow, the lobster has to shed its shell from time to time.

Jointed abdomen can bend and move inside its flexible armor.

Jointed walking leg – there are four pairs of these.

11

Single shells

Mollusks with their shell in one piece are called gastropods, or snails. The shell usually coils in a spiral around the body and has a wide opening at one end. The snail can push its head and foot out of this opening, while the rest of the body stays hidden safely inside.

Belly-foot

The word *gastropod* means "belly-foot." We think of the snail's large, flat, creeping foot as the belly of the animal.

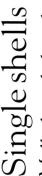

Empty home

Look out for this typical gastropod shell on the beach. It is the empty home of a whelk – a type of sea snail. It has thick ridges on the outside and coils in a clockwise direction from the tip down to the wide, open part.

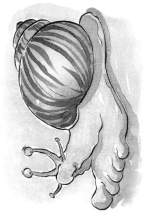

Tip of shell

Shell is patterned with ridges

Bottom, largest whorl, or turn, of shell

Opening through which whelk pushes out its body

Groove through which whelk pokes out its siphon (see right).

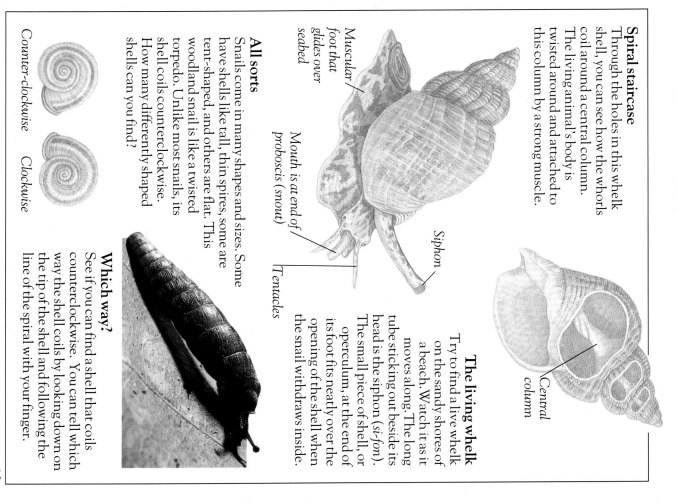

Spiral staircase

Through the holes in this whelk shell, you can see how the whorls coil around a central column. The living animal's body is twisted around and attached to this column by a strong muscle.

Muscular foot that glides over seabed

Mouth is at end of proboscis (snout)

Siphon

Tentacles

Central column

All sorts

Snails come in many shapes and sizes. Some have shells like tall, thin spires, some are tent-shaped, and others are flat. This woodland snail is like a twisted torpedo. Unlike most snails, its shell coils counterclockwise. How many differently shaped shells can you find?

Counter-clockwise

Clockwise

The living whelk

Try to find a live whelk on the sandy shores of a beach. Watch it as it moves along. The long tube sticking out beside its head is the siphon (si-fon). The small piece of shell, or operculum, at the end of its foot fits neatly over the opening of the shell when the snail withdraws inside.

Which way?

See if you can find a shell that coils counterclockwise. You can tell which way the shell coils by looking down on the tip of the shell and following the line of the spiral with your finger.

13

Double shells

Mollusks with two shells are called bivalves. The two shells (valves) are joined together at one side by a hinge. The living animal inside can hold both valves tightly together with two strong muscles, but it can also open its valves to feed and breathe. Most bivalves live in the sea.

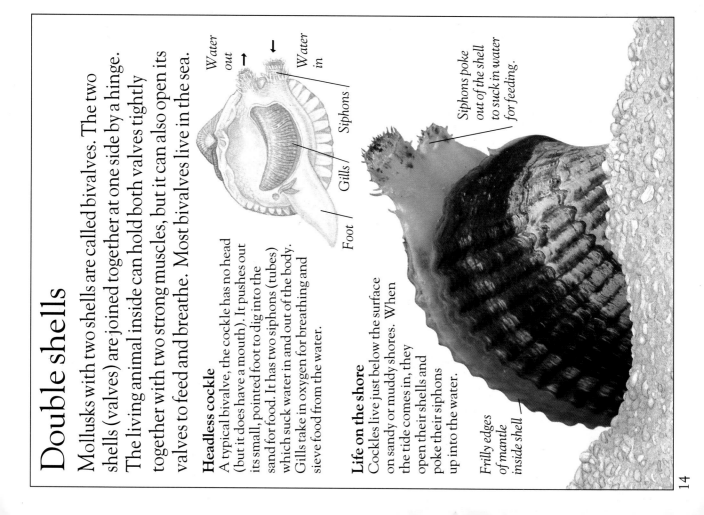

Water out

Water in

Siphons

Gills

Foot

Headless cockle

A typical bivalve, the cockle has no head (but it does have a mouth). It pushes out its small, pointed foot to dig into the sand for food. It has two siphons (tubes) which suck water in and out of the body. Gills take in oxygen for breathing and sieve food from the water.

Life on the shore

Cockles live just below the surface on sandy or muddy shores. When the tide comes in, they open their shells and poke their siphons up into the water.

Siphons poke out of the shell to suck in water for feeding.

Frilly edges of mantle inside shell

14

Cockle cracker

Cockles and mussels should beware of the orange bill of the oystercatcher! This bird hammers open bivalve shells, then snips out the juicy creature inside. Oystercatchers can eat up to 300 cockles in one day.

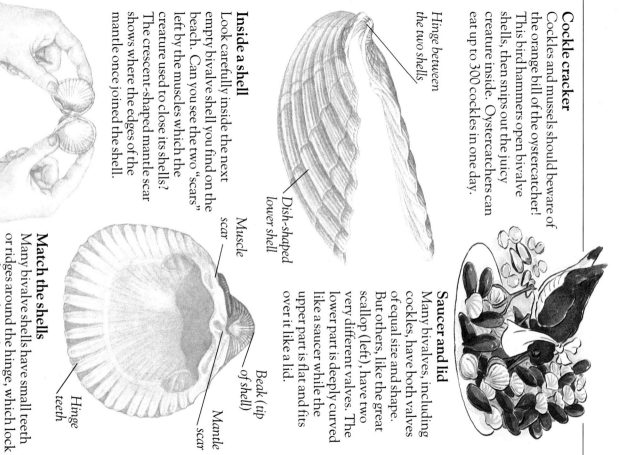

Hinge between the two shells

Dish-shaped lower shell

Saucer and lid

Many bivalves, including cockles, have both valves of equal size and shape. But others, like the great scallop (left), have two very different valves. The lower part is deeply curved like a saucer while the upper part is flat and fits over it like a lid.

Inside a shell

Look carefully inside the next empty bivalve shell you find on the beach. Can you see the two "scars" left by the muscles which the creature used to close its shells? The crescent-shaped mantle scar shows where the edges of the mantle once joined the shell.

Muscle scar

Beak (tip of shell)

Mantle scar

Hinge teeth

Match the shells

Many bivalve shells have small teeth or ridges around the hinge, which lock together with notches in the opposite shell. Can you find two matching shells that fit together tightly?

Collecting shells

Why not start your own shell collection? Pick up empty shells from woods, parks, fields, and gardens; near ponds and streams; and at the seashore. Take some small boxes and plastic bags with you, and put each shell into a separate box or bag. Remember to note down where and when you found your empty shells.

Sea in a shell

If you hold a large seashell up to your ear and listen hard, you should be able to hear the sound of the waves on some distant shore.

All sorts of shells

Separate the shells you find into different groups so you can label them easily. You might decide to keep seashells, land shells, and freshwater shells in three separate boxes. Or you may want to mix up shells from different places in one box (right).

Seashells

Land shells

Freshwater shells

Some shells are very thin and fragile, so handle them with care.

Cleaning your shells

Wash your shells in warm, soapy water. If they are very dirty or encrusted with weeds, scrub them gently with a nail brush, or a soft toothbrush. Rinse the shells in cold water, then leave them to dry on newspaper.

16

Make a display box

You can make an attractive display box for your shells. You will need six big empty matchboxes, glue, cotton wool, scissors, thin cardboard, and a pen.

1 Glue six large matchboxes together, side by side. Now glue the two rows together. Each matchbox has two sections. Your display box should now have 12 sections.

2 Put a layer of cotton wool into each section of your display box.

3 Carefully cut out rectangles of cardboard for labels. Fold them in half and glue them to one wall of each section. Now put your shells into the display case.

"Garden snails found under stone, March 6th"

"Cockle found on sandy beach, August 1st"

Shells with legs

Crabs, shrimps, prawns, and lobsters belong to a group of animals called crustaceans (*crust-ay-shuns*). Their bodies are covered with a tough shell made of separate segments joined together by flexible joints. These allow the body and legs to bend. From time to time, crustaceans have to shed their shells in order to grow.

Segments allow the body to bend

Leaping prawns
Prawns have much thinner shells than crabs and lobsters. They can shoot backward by flicking their tails under their bodies.

Ancient but agile
Lobsters may live for up to 100 years! Even at this ripe old age, they can suddenly leap backward with a strong flick of their tail.

On the move
Every year, huge numbers of these spiny lobsters move from shallow seas into deeper waters to escape the winter storms. They march across the seabed in columns of up to 60, keeping in line by feeling each other with their antennae.

Antennae are spiny

Strong pincer claws
can grip tightly

Short and fat

You can recognize the squat lobster by its massive front claws, which are twice as long as its body. By contrast, its last pair of walking legs are very small and are hidden under the body. The squat lobster tucks its tail under its body most of the time.

Back pair of jointed legs are shaped like oars to allow the crab to swim

Velvet swimming crab

Keep a look out in tide pools for the velvet swimming crab. It has bright red eyes and velvety hairs on its shell. Like most crabs, it has two strong pincer claws and a broad, flattened body. It catches fish and other prey by swimming rapidly sideways.

This lobster has lost its front right walking leg. Can you see the new leg growing?

Crafty crabs

Most crabs are well protected by their heavily armored shells and sharp pincers. But some only have thin shells and need to find special homes to live in. Other crabs have developed extra special ways of defending themselves.

Hermit crab

A hermit crab has no shell on its back. Although the crab has tough pincers at the front, its back end has only a soft outer skin. The crab solves this problem by living in an empty mollusk shell.

A sea anemone often hitches a ride on the hermit crab's home. When open, (right), its stinging tentacles help protect the crab from enemies.

A whelk shell makes a welcome home for this large hermit crab.

The crab withdraws completely into the shell, guarding the entrance with its pincers.

Moving house

A hermit crab eventually grows too big for its home. It looks around for a bigger shell, which it explores carefully with its pincers and antennae. It moves in quickly, tail first, before anything can attack its soft, pink body.

Tiny pea crab inside mussel shell

Pea crab

Not much bigger than a pea, this harmless thin-shelled crab lives inside a bivalve. It steals tiny bits of food sucked in by the bivalve.

Crab search

Look out for different kinds of crabs on the beach. Crabs often hide under stones. To pick one up safely, hold each side of the shell between finger and thumb.

Crabs can give nasty nips. Keep your fingers away from the pincers.

Boxing gloves

This crafty crab adds to its defense system by carrying an anemone on the end of each claw. If a fish tries to attack the crab, it receives a bunch of stinging tentacles in the face!

Male crab has three segments

Male or female?

You can tell what sex a crab is by looking underneath its body. The male's tail flap is narrow and pointed, with three segments. A female has a wider tail flap with more segments.

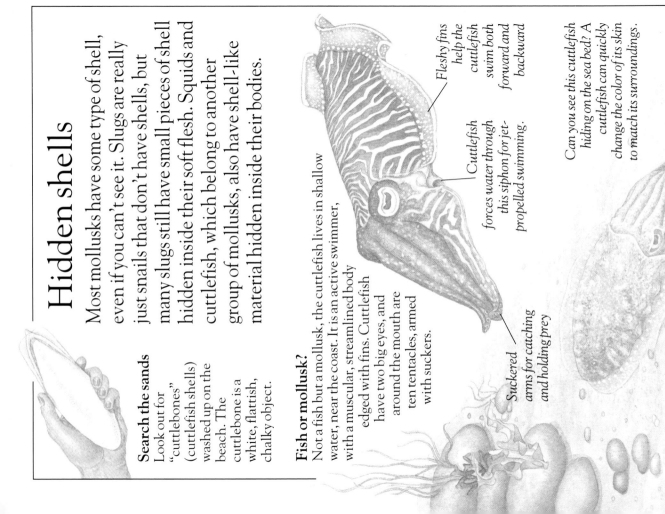

Hidden shells

Most mollusks have some type of shell, even if you can't see it. Slugs are really just snails that don't have shells, but many slugs still have small pieces of shell hidden inside their soft flesh. Squids and cuttlefish, which belong to another group of mollusks, also have shell-like material hidden inside their bodies.

Search the sands
Look out for "cuttlebones" (cuttlefish shells) washed up on the beach. The cuttlebone is a white, flattish, chalky object.

Fish or mollusk?
Not a fish but a mollusk, the cuttlefish lives in shallow water, near the coast. It is an active swimmer, with a muscular, streamlined body edged with fins. Cuttlefish have two big eyes, and around the mouth are ten tentacles, armed with suckers.

Fleshy fins help the cuttlefish swim both forward and backward

Cuttlefish forces water through this siphon for jet-propelled swimming.

Suckered arms for catching and holding prey

Can you see this cuttlefish hiding on the sea bed? A cuttlefish can quickly change the color of its skin to match its surroundings.

22

Speedy squid

Shaped like torpedoes, squids can swim very fast. Like cuttlefish, they avoid danger by darting suddenly backward by jet propulsion, forcing water out of the siphon underneath the head. If frightened, they can also squirt a cloud of ink into the water to distract their attacker.

Slug or snail?

This worm-eating land slug has a tiny shell, but this shell would not be much good at defending it from predators. Can you see the coiling at the tip of the shell?

Slug with ears

The sea hare gets its name from the long earlike tentacles sticking up from its head like hare's ears. This soft, fleshy mollusk is a type of sea slug, but it has a thin, transparent shell hidden beneath the folds of its mantle.

Earlike tentacles

Fleshy folds of mantle that hide the inner shell

Spiny shells

Sea urchins are shells with a difference. Hundreds of sharp, movable spines cover the hard test (shell) that hides the urchin's soft body. Like a porcupine, the sea urchin needs its spiny armor to protect itself from enemies. It also uses its spines to move around on the sea bed and to burrow into rocks or sand.

Stiff, movable spines

Sensitive tube feet stretch out to feel around for food.

Mouth with five beaklike jaws (now closed) on body

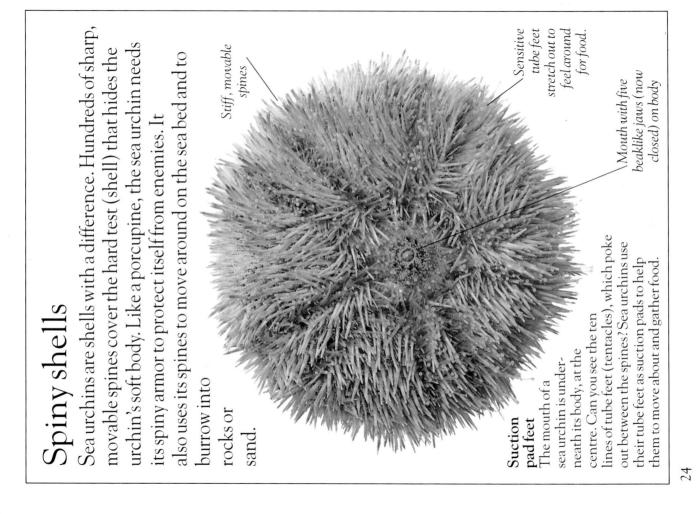

Suction pad feet

The mouth of a sea urchin is underneath its body, at the centre. Can you see the ten lines of tube feet (tentacles), which poke out between the spines? Sea urchins use their tube feet as suction pads to help them to move about and gather food.

Moving jaws

Here is a sea urchin's mouth in close-up. When it feeds, the five jaws open and close to crunch or nibble at seaweed and barnacles covering the rocks.

Once a sea urchin dies, its spines fall off.

Sea urchin spines can cut your feet – so wear shoes if you go snorkeling near them!

Slate pencil urchin

The slate pencil urchin is one of the largest sea urchins in the world. Its test is as big as a grapefruit. It lives on coral reefs and uses its heavy, clublike spines to wedge itself into crevices safe from pounding waves.

Test search

Look for empty sea urchin tests washed up on the beach. You may find the fragile heart-shaped test of a burrowing heart urchin. The rows of holes show where the tube feet poked out through the test.

Fancy dress

Sea urchins living close to the shore often cover themselves with bits of shell, stones, or seaweed. They pick these pieces up with their tube feet and hold them in place to act as a sunshade or disguise from predators.

25

Reptiles with shells

Tortoises, turtles, and terrapins have lived on Earth since the time of the dinosaurs. They have changed little since then. A hard bony shell encases the animal's soft body. This shell is fixed to the animal's skeleton. The outside of the shell is covered with a layer of tough, horny plates, made of the same material as your fingernails.

Slow but steady

If you carried a shell as heavy as the one a tortoise carries, you would move slowly too. But in the old story *The Tortoise and the Hare*, the speedy hare lost the race. He stopped for a nap, while the tortoise plodded on past him, and won!

Starry disguise

The beautiful star-shaped markings on this starred tortoise are not only decorative. They help camouflage the animal in the dry African grassland where it lives.

Domed shell is difficult for predators to grab hold of

Head and legs can tuck under shell for safety

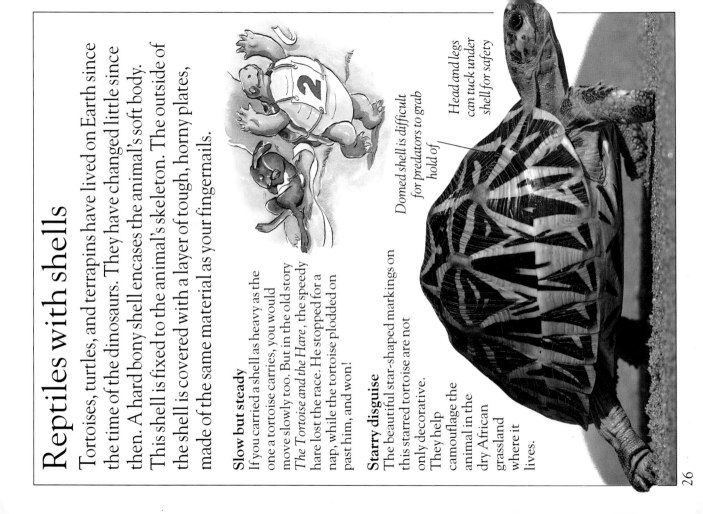

Red ears

Can you tell the difference between a tortoise and a terrapin? Terrapins live in freshwater, and their shells are flatter than tortoise shells. The red-eared terrapin has a bright red blob on each side of its head.

Snapping with death

Beware the vicious jaws of the North American snapping turtle! It sometimes attacks swimmers and will eat almost anything. It is an expert at sniffing out dead flesh – including human corpses in swamps and lakes.

Powerful paddlers

Sea turtles have lighter shells than tortoises. They are graceful swimmers and use their strong, paddlelike flippers like underwater wings. The loggerhead turtle (left) has powerful jaws for crushing the shells of crabs, mollusks, and other prey.

Beach birth

Sea turtles come ashore to lay their eggs on warm, sandy beaches. The female turtle digs a hole, lays up to 100 eggs, then covers them with sand. Several weeks later, the baby turtles hatch out.

Baby turtles race down to the sea after hatching.

🐾 *Never disturb eggs or baby turtles on the beach!*

How shells are born

Most land snails lay eggs in the ground that hatch into baby snails. Pond snails and some sea snails lay their eggs in a mass of jelly, which they stick to weeds and stones underwater. Other sea snails produce eggs in leathery cases. And most bivalves release millions of eggs into the sea. These eggs hatch into tiny creatures called larvae, which settle on the bottom and grow into adult mollusks.

The snails produce a lot of slime as they press the soles of their feet together.

Love darts

Some land snails court each other before mating by shooting tiny, chalky darts into each others' bodies.

Snails entwined

Most land snails are both male and female. But two snails still need to mate before they can lay eggs. The mating snails do a courtship dance before pressing their bodies together in a mass of slime.

28

Watching eggs hatch

Why not collect some snail eggs and watch them hatching out yourself?

1 Search under rotting leaves or logs to find a batch of snail's eggs. Put them into a jar on top of some damp soil. Cover the jar with a piece of cloth and leave it in a cool, dark place. Wait a week or two for the snails to hatch.

2 Give your baby snails some lettuce leaves to eat. Watch them grow for a week or so, then let them go, to find their own food.

Eggs in the ground

Garden snails lay up to 50 pearly white eggs in a small hole in the soil or under rotting leaves, logs, or stones.

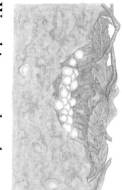

Use a magnifying glass to look at the baby snails. Can you see their thin, transparent shells?

Egg necklace

The necklace shell lays its eggs in a coiled ribbon of slime that becomes coated with sand and then hardens into a stiff, necklace-like collar. The eggs often hatch into tiny larvae before growing into snails.

Adult necklace shell on sandy shore

Stiff "necklace" of eggs coated in sand

The growing shell

Mollusks make their own shells. As the animal grows, the hard shell grows with it. The part of the mollusk that makes the shell is called the mantle. This is a cloak of skin that covers the mollusk's body. When the weather is bad, or there is no food, the animal stops growing for awhile. This gives the shell uneven lines of growth.

Chalk eaters

Mollusks need to make strong shells to protect their soft bodies from predators. Land snails must live where there is plenty of calcium, which makes their shells hard. They find calcium in chalk or limestone. Many snails actually swallow tiny bits of chalk in their food. Sea snails get their calcium from seawater.

Growing gradually

These pictures show how a star turban shell grows. The young shell has only two or three coils and is very spiky. As it grows, the snail adds more shell around the rim, making more and bigger coils around its body. The spikes are gradually worn away.

Young shell

Spikes

Shell has only two or three coils

Older shell

Fully grown shell

Mouth of shell where new shell is added

Knobbly lines on shell – spines have worn away

First year's growth is at tip of the shell

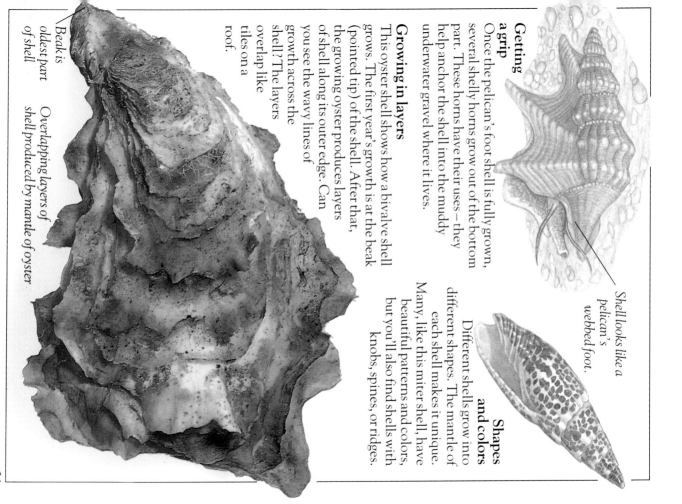

Getting a grip

Once the pelican's foot shell is fully grown, several shelly horns grow out of the bottom part. These horns have their uses — they help anchor the shell into the muddy underwater gravel where it lives.

Growing in layers

This oyster shell shows how a bivalve shell grows. The first year's growth is at the beak (pointed tip) of the shell. After that, the growing oyster produces layers of shell along its outer edge. Can you see the wavy lines of growth across the shell? The layers overlap like tiles on a roof.

Shell looks like a pelican's webbed foot.

Shapes and colors

Different shells grow into different shapes. The mantle of each shell makes it unique. Many, like this miter shell, have beautiful patterns and colors, but you'll also find shells with knobs, spines, or ridges.

Beak is oldest part of shell

Overlapping layers of shell produced by mantle of oyster

Giant shells

Few shelled mollusks grow bigger than about four inches, and some are smaller than a grain of sand! But there are some giants, too. These mostly come from warm tropical waters. Their large, empty shells are often used by the local people as water containers, trumpets, or even bathtubs.

Starfish-eater
In real life, this giant triton is twice the size of the land snail below. It lives in Australia, on the Great Barrier Reef, where it feeds on the crown-of-thorns starfish.

Land monster
If you live in Africa, you may see this monster crawling around in your garden! The giant African snail – which is actually as big as this picture shows – is very fond of garden plants and some crops.

Long tentacle has an eye at the tip.

Short tentacles have no eyes but are used for feeling and smelling.

32

Sea monster

With a shell up to five feet long, the giant clam is the world's largest bivalve. This clam lives on reefs, wedged among rocks and coral. The shells gape open most of the time.

Fleshy lobes of mantle

Bath time

If you visit the Indo-Pacific islands, you might find yourself bathing in a giant clam's shell! The islanders eat the clam's flesh and use the shells as tubs and troughs.

An ordinary garden snail shows you the difference in size of the two animals.

The large bottom whorl is the youngest part of the snail's coiled shell.

Grazers and browsers

Most land snails and freshwater snails are herbivores, or plant-eaters. They are especially fond of dead and rotting vegetation. Some seashore snails are herbivores too – they eat different kinds of seaweed. All these snails have a long radula, or tongue, which is covered with tiny sharp teeth that grate, cut, and tear up the plant food.

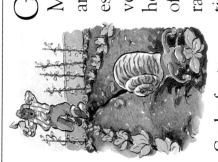

Garden feast
Snails can be a nuisance in the garden. They love to eat the tender shoots of young plants.

Browsing on moss
Many snails nibble at moss and lichens growing on tree bark. Slowly the snail stretches out its body to explore the tree trunk. It uses its mouth and the two small tentacles on its head to search out food by touch, smell, and taste.

Moss growing on tree trunk

34

Sandpaper tongue

A snail can have between 15,000 and 50,000 teeth on its tongue — depending on what kind of snail it is. The tongue acts like sandpaper as it scrapes off bits of food.

Fleshy lobes around mouth cling onto weeds

Pond snails have only one pair of tentacles with an eye at the bottom of each.

Great pond snail

Look out for this snail in ponds and slow-flowing rivers. It feeds mainly on water weeds and tiny plants called algae. You may see it come to the surface to take in air.

Homing limpets

The next time you are at the beach, search for limpets on algae-covered rocks. Follow these steps to see just how they graze on the algae.

1 Mark a limpet's shell with nail polish. Continue the mark down onto the rock. You will now be able to tell if the limpet returns to the same spot after feeding.

Tracks made by limpet's tongue as it scraped off algae growing on the rock.

2 The next day, go back to check the position of your limpet. Has it returned to the same spot? Can you see any feeding tracks around it?

Flesh eaters

Animals that eat flesh are called carnivores. Some are active hunters – they kill their prey. Others, called scavengers, feed on dead or injured animals. Many sea snails are carnivorous. A sea snail's mouth is at the end of a long tube that it uses to probe inside the shells and bodies of other animals. Sea snails also have sharp teeth on their tongues for piercing flesh.

Special probes detect the slime trails of its prey.

These South Pacific island Partula snails are a favorite meal for the Euglandina!

Killer on land

Most land snails eat plants, but this Euglandina (*You-glan-dina*) snail is a carnivore. It eats other snails, using its long, sharp teeth to tear up their flesh. Once onto the trail of a meal, the Euglandina moves quickly, stretching out its body to grasp its victim.

Pretty, but deadly

Cone shells are among the deadliest of sea snails. Their sharp, harpoon-like teeth are loaded with paralyzing poison. When a fish comes too close, the cone sinks a tooth into it and injects the poison. It then swallows the fish whole.

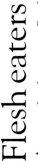
Never pick up a living cone shell. Some of them can kill people.

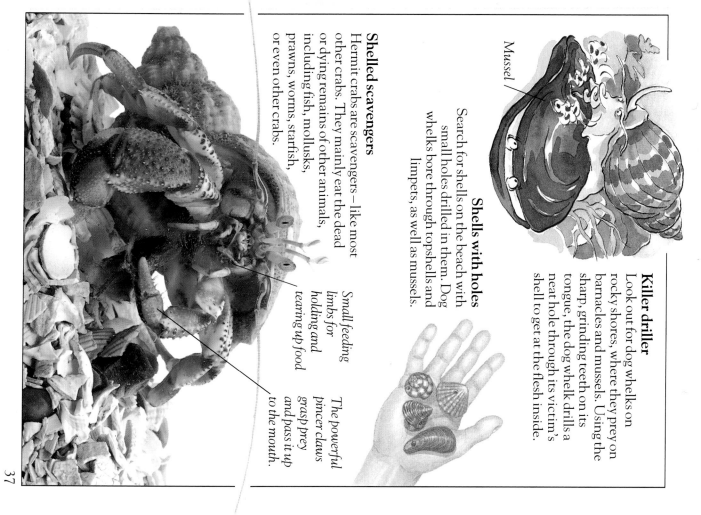

Killer driller

Look out for dog whelks on rocky shores, where they prey on barnacles and mussels. Using the sharp, grinding teeth on its tongue, the dog whelk drills a neat hole through its victim's shell to get at the flesh inside.

Mussel

Shells with holes

Search for shells on the beach with small holes drilled in them. Dog whelks bore through topshells and limpets, as well as mussels.

Shelled scavengers

Hermit crabs are scavengers – like most other crabs. They mainly eat the dead or dying remains of other animals, including fish, mollusks, prawns, worms, starfish, or even other crabs.

Small feeding limbs for holding and tearing up food

The powerful pincer claws grasp prey and pass it up to the mouth.

37

Filter feeders

All bivalves and some gastropod sea snails are filter feeders. Like mini vacuum cleaners, they suck a stream of water into one opening and push it out through another. Inside the shell's body, sievelike gills trap tiny plants and animals that are in the water. Some filter feeders suck up food from the seabed instead.

Sieving the sea

Seawater is packed with millions of tiny floating animals and plants, called plankton. This is the food that filter feeders trap and pass to their stomachs when they suck streams of water into their bodies.

Living dangerously

When covered by the tide, a mussel opens its shells and begins to pump water in and out of its body. If the water is polluted, it filters in poisons. They collect in the bodies of the mussels and can make them dangerous for humans to eat.

Smooth opening pushes out waste water

Frilly opening sucks in water and food

Feeling for food

Believe it or not, barnacles are crustaceans, like crabs. A shrimplike animal lives inside each hard barnacle shell. When the tide comes in, the animal pokes out its feathery legs and combs plankton from the water.

Look for sand gaper siphons hidden in seaweed – they are often bitten off by hungry fish.

Shorter siphon pumps out waste water.

Long siphon sweeps over sand and "vacuums" up bits of food.

Sand gaper

The sand gaper lives buried as deep as 16 inches below the sand. Its two siphons join up into one fat tube that stretches to the surface to collect the animal's food from the water.

Muscular foot helps the gaper to burrow.

Sucking up

Tellin shells burrow in muddy sand. They feed by pushing two tubes, called siphons, up above the surface. If you find a tellin, carefully put it in a shaded container of seawater – it will extend its siphons if you leave it alone.

The thick siphon tube forces the two shells to gape open – hence the name sand gaper.

Traveling shells

Most mollusks move slowly. Snails creep, glide, or shuffle along on a muscular foot. Some sea snails may use a part of their shell to dig into the surface; others have an enormous foot that plows through the sand like a bulldozer. Bivalves mainly dig or burrow into the sand.

Swimming scallops

When scallops need to move quickly, they clap their shells together like a pair of castanets. This clapping forces water out from between the shell, and pushes the scallop forward and upward. This movement is called jet propulsion.

Jet propulsion pushes the scallop up and away

Starfish love eating scallops; they force the bivalve shells apart with tiny suckered feet.

Scallop rests on the seabed with both valves almost closed.

Sensitive tentacles and eyespots

40

Leaping from danger

When faced with a predator, some types of mollusk leap away! They dig their powerful foot into the sand, then straighten it suddenly, to flick themselves away. You do the same when you crouch your body before you dive into a swimming pool.

Slime time

As it moves along, the snail's foot produces a trail of sticky slime. This helps it cling the surface and glide along smoothly.

Watch a snail's trails

You can find out exactly how a snail moves along by watching its underside through glass.

1 Find a garden snail and put it carefully into a jam jar. Look closely at the bottom of its foot as it climbs up the sides.

2 Watch the bands of muscles in its foot. Can you see the ripple movements as the muscles lift each part of the foot in turn? Notice how the snail moves its tentacles.

Tentacles

Mouth

Glistening trail of slime allows the snail to travel over rough, sharp surfaces.

Bands of muscle across the foot help push the snail forward.

41

Clinging on

Living underwater can be difficult. In some rivers, water rushes by quickly, while on the seabed waves and currents pound against the shore. Many shelled animals survive by clinging tightly to rocks, seaweed, or other shells. Some fix themselves to one spot for life. They rely on currents in the water to bring them food.

Shells upon shells

This small group of hard-shelled sea creatures are clinging tightly to a limpet shell, which itself is clinging to a rock. At high tide the limpet will move slowly over the rocks to feed on seaweed, while the hitchhikers on its shell will filter food from the water.

Barnacles cement themselves to a hard surface as young larvae before building their outer cases and settling down for life.

Slipper limpet clings on with its muscular foot and filters food from the sea

Limpet shell provides a firm surface for clinging on

A tubeworm has cemented its chalky white tube to the limpet shell

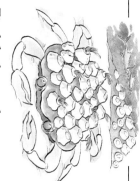

Fan mussel

Mussels attach themselves to the seabed with long, sticky threads called byssus threads. The threads harden in water and hold the shell firmly in place like the ropes of a tent. This big fan mussel sits upright in the water.

Find the barnacles

Young barnacles settle and attach themselves to all kinds of hard surfaces, including rocks, mollusk shells, crabs, or even boats. Search around on rocky shores and make a list of the different objects that barnacles cling to.

Cemented to the spot

Oysters live on the bottom of rivers or the seabed. They fix their shell to the bottom by pouring out a sticky substance which hardens like cement and fixes them firmly in place.

Flexible shell of eight over-lapping plates

Armor-plated chitons are often called coat-of-mail shells.

Curling shell

When the tide is out, chitons clamp themselves tightly to the rocks with a suction-cup foot. The chiton's shell has eight movable parts. If it is knocked off a rock, the chiton can curl up to protect itself.

Defense tactics

You might think that shelled animals are well-protected inside their hard outer cases – but a shell alone isn't always enough. Some animals threaten their enemies or hide themselves away. Others blend into the background to fool hungry hunters.

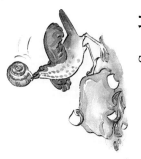

Smash!

The song-thrush has a special stone called its anvil, on which it smashes open the shells of garden snails. Then it eats the soft animal inside.

Male crabs have an extra-large pincer claw

Nimble legs for escaping quickly

Crab alert

Crabs have many enemies, including fish, octopuses, gulls, and other seabirds. When threatened, this Caribbean land crab rears up on its back legs, waving and snapping its powerful pincers in warning.

Hairy mouthful

Most snails protect themselves from attack by pulling their bodies safely back inside their shells. Some also block the mouth of the shell with their operculum. But the hairy snail has an extra weapon – a rough, bristly shell that predators find horrible to eat.

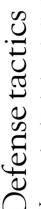

Living sponges grow on shell

Stuck to a spot

Imagine you were glued to the ground – how would you defend yourself? Oysters are stuck to one place, and they rely on clever disguises for protection. This thorny oyster is so well-disguised with sponges and seaweed on its shell that predators usually ignore it.

Mouth of shell

Rubbery part between the two hinged valves

A mouthful of spines

Look for spiny oysters attached to rock or coral. Their thick heavy shells are covered with sturdy spines. Hungry fish, crabs or starfish find the spines too much of a mouthful and leave the animal alone.

Snap happy

When danger threatens, the spiny oyster snaps its valves together tightly and relies on its thick, spiny shell to protect it from harm. Starfish simply can't get to the tasty animal inside.

Jewels from the sea

Beneath the ocean is a world of hidden treasures. Seashells strung together or carved make beautiful necklaces, bracelets, ornaments, and brooches. The most precious shelly jewels, pearls, are made inside mollusk shells, such as oysters.

Blister pearl

Pearly lining of shell (called mother-of-pearl)

Blister pearl

If an annoying piece of grit or little creature gets inside an oyster or other mollusk shell, a pearl begins to be born. This blister pearl has formed on the surface of a black-lipped oyster shell.

Perfect pearls

Perfectly round pearls are very rare. An oyster makes them on the inner side of its mantle.

How a blister pearl is formed

The oyster's mantle begins to cover the grit with shelly material called mother-of-pearl.

Gradually, the mantle adds more layers of pearl around the grit until the pearl sticks out as a bump.

After a few years, the pearl may grow big enough to break away from the shell.

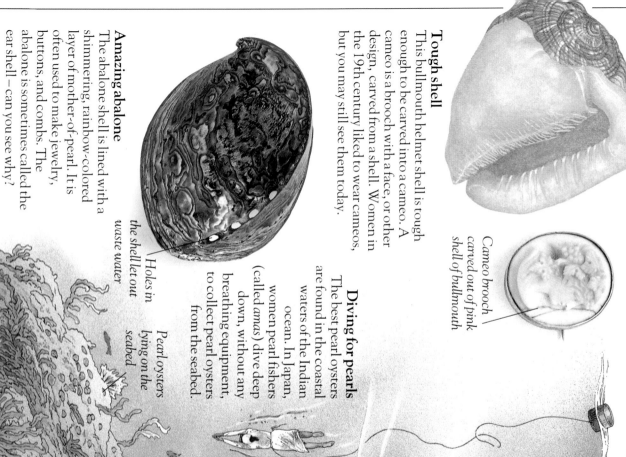

Tough shell

This bullmouth helmet shell is tough enough to be carved into a cameo. A cameo is a brooch with a face, or other design, carved from a shell. Women in the 19th century liked to wear cameos, but you may still see them today.

Cameo brooch carved out of pink shell of bullmouth

Amazing abalone

The abalone shell is lined with a shimmering, rainbow-colored layer of mother-of-pearl. It is often used to make jewelry, buttons, and combs. The abalone is sometimes called the ear shell – can you see why?

Holes in the shell let out waste water

Diving for pearls

The best pearl oysters are found in the coastal waters of the Indian ocean. In Japan, women pearl fishers (called *amas*) dive deep down, without any breathing equipment, to collect pearl oysters from the seabed.

Pearl oysters lying on the seabed

47

Shells on land

If you are looking for shells on land, you are most likely to find snails. Gardens and fields, woods and forests, mountains, and even deserts are home to some type of snail. Snails need to keep their bodies moist, so they are happiest in damp, shady places. They come out to feed mainly at night. Some crabs from hot countries live on land, but they need to return to the sea to have their young.

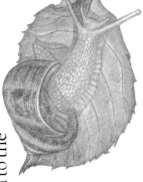

No sea in sight
A crab that lives on land sounds like a joke, but this blue land crab can live many miles inland. It digs burrows in the ground for shelter and can climb trees to search for food.

Garden snail
Look out for the garden snail in parks and gardens. Its shell has dark bands on it that blend in with its background.

Forest snail
Snails love the cool, damp climate of woods and forests. They can live and feed among the dead leaves on the forest floor; they can climb up trees to find food and shelter. This snail lives in Australian forests.

Hibernating snails

In colder countries, snails hibernate in winter so that they don't freeze to death. Some seal themselves to stones. Others withdraw inside their shells and seal the opening with a thick plug of hardened slime. They sleep for several months. Can you find some hibernating snails in the park or garden?

Whitish plug seals the snail inside its shell.

Snails on trees

Tree snails live in countries that have a warm, moist climate, so they don't need to worry about freezing to death. The snails spend most of their time grazing on algae and lichens on the trunks of trees.

Tree snails are often big and colorful – these are life size.

49

Freshwater shells

Ponds, lakes, streams, and rivers are home to lots of shelled animals. Gastropod snails cling and creep over weeds and stones. Bivalves such as freshwater mussels and oysters lie half-buried in the mud or silt on the bottom, and small shrimplike animals are everywhere. You'll find freshwater crabs and crayfish in certain rivers, as well as freshwater turtles and terrapins if you live in a warm country.

When in danger, the turtle bends its long neck back along its body and tucks in its head.

Turtle neck

This freshwater turtle lives in the rivers of Australia. It pokes its long, flexible neck among the rocks to hunt out fish, shrimps, and snails. Its webbed feet and smooth, streamlined shape make it a good swimmer.

Hidden hunter

Freshwater crayfish are small spiny lobsters. They live in fast-flowing streams and hide away by day under stones or in holes in the bank. They hunt mainly by night, catching their prey – snails, water insects, or fish – in their pincers.

Dipping for shells

Look for shells in a pond or stream by dipping with a net. Sweep your net slowly through the weeds, then gently turn it inside out into a tub of water. You can search through the weeds for shelled animals.

Take special care by the water – you could fall in!

Gasping for air

Some freshwater snails can breathe underwater, but giant pond snails need to breathe oxygen from the air. They come to the surface every now and then to take in a gulp of air through a hole in their mantle.

Sticky zebras

Zebra mussels hang onto hard objects such as underwater stones and posts, with fine, sticky threads. Large clumps of zebra mussels often live in water pipes and canals. They sometimes clog the pipes and block the flow of water.

Snorkeling snails

Apple snails live in warm muddy swamps where there is little oxygen in the water for breathing. They get fresh air by pushing a long tube up to the surface – like you snorkeling in the sea!

Sandy shore shells

Sandy shores may look empty of life. There are no rocks or seaweeds for animals to cling to or hide under. But a look underneath the sand will reveal a whole world of creatures. Burrowing bivalves stay mostly hidden, and push up tubes to the surface to feed and breathe. Hiding crabs and shrimps come out to feed at night.

Once buried, the razor shell filters food from the sea through its short siphons.

Shell pulls itself upright

Digging foot

Foot swelling

Life in the sand

Most sandy shore shells live near the lowest point on the beach reached by the tide. They rely on the sea to rush in and bring them fresh supplies of food and oxygen.

Into the sand

The razor shell, a bivalve, has a smooth, flattened shell which slides easily through the sand. It can dig so fast it's impossible to catch one. First the foot digs down, then it swells up to grip the sand while tightening muscles pull the shell below the surface.

Pelican's foot shell

This shallow water dweller may use its jagged shell to secure itself in the sand. It probes for food with its long, snoutlike proboscis.

Knobbly spiral shell

Below the tideline

Wentletrap shells and many other gastropods live below the tideline. But wentletraps lay their eggs close to the shore, near sea anemones, on which they feed.

Tall and thin spiral shell

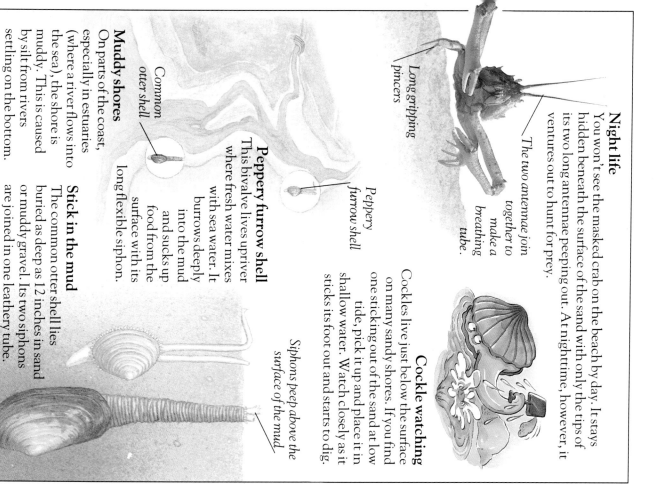

Night life

You won't see the masked crab on the beach by day. It stays hidden beneath the surface of the sand with only the tips of its two long antennae peeping out. At nighttime, however, it ventures out to hunt for prey.

Long gripping pincers

The two antennae join together to make a breathing tube.

Cockle watching

Cockles live just below the surface on many sandy shores. If you find one sticking out of the sand at low tide, pick it up and place it in shallow water. Watch closely as it sticks its foot out and starts to dig.

Siphons peep above the surface of the mud

Peppery furrow shell

This bivalve lives upriver where fresh water mixes with sea water. It burrows deeply into the mud and sucks up food from the surface with its long flexible siphon.

Peppery furrow shell

Common otter shell

Muddy shores

On parts of the coast, especially in estuaries (where a river flows into the sea), the shore is muddy. This is caused by silt from rivers settling on the bottom.

Stick in the mud

The common otter shell lies buried as deep as 12 inches in sand or muddy gravel. Its two siphons are joined in one leathery tube.

Rocky shore shells

From a distance, a rocky shore might look like just stones and water. But take a closer look – rocky shores are packed with different shelled inhabitants. Limpets and other mollusks cling to the rocks or seaweed; and when the tide goes out, crabs hide in damp crevices, and sea urchins and prawns shelter in tide pools.

Trapped for life
Piddocks burrow into the rock and stay there for life. When the tide is in, they poke their siphons out to filter feed.

This is how piddocks look inside the rock.

Shutting up shop
If left high and dry by the tide, limpets clasp the rock tightly and barnacles simply close up their shells.

Life in the pool
When the tide goes out, many shells become trapped in tide pools. A shady tide pool is a good place to watch shells – a minihabitat for you to observe, without swimming out to sea!

A sea anemone opens out its tentacles to feed.

Short-armed cushion star

Small prawns are often eaten by sea anemones.

Can you spot the sea urchin hiding under its seaweed camouflage?

A world of periwinkles

Different kinds of winkles live at every level of the shore. Rough periwinkles hide in crevices. Edible periwinkles, the biggest, come lower down. Flat periwinkles can be found on seaweed.

Flat periwinkles feed on fucus seaweed.

Shore crabs are not fussy eaters — they will eat almost anything.

Rough periwinkle

Edible periwinkle

Plastic wrap

Plastic pipe

Dog whelks

Carnivorous dog whelks prey on barnacles and mussels. Look for their yellow egg cases tucked away in rock crevices.

Take care not to fall in – jagged rocks can hurt!

Underwater view

Take a closer look at tide pool life by making an underwater viewer. Cover one end of a piece of wide plastic pipe with plastic wrap. Put on a rubber band to hold it in place. Hold your viewer just below the surface and look through the open end. Stay very still and watch the underwater action.

Crab in the dark

Watch your fingers if you pick up stones or seaweed! A common shore crab may be hiding there. The shore crab's dark green shell blends in with the tide pool, hiding it from predators such as seagulls.

Warm water shells

You are likely to see some of the biggest and brightest sea shells in the warm, tropical waters of the world. Around coral reefs, the warm shallow water is home to many colorful mollusks, shrimps, and crabs. The water is full of plant life, and the coral provides food and shelter for the animals.

Murex shell

Well armed with spines, knobs, and frilly branches, this shell belongs to a sea snail which feeds on bivalves and barnacles. The murex shell lives among rocks and coral in tropical seas.

Long curving spike carries the snail's siphon

Scorpion conch

This shell looks like a scorpion. The spikes may help to anchor it firmly in the sand, while the long curved spike at the front end, looking like a scorpion's tail, carries the mollusk's siphon.

Painted prawn

Lots of prawns and shrimps live in the nooks and crannies of a coral reef. They come out mainly at night to search for food. This painted prawn, recognizable by its spotty pattern, is carrying off a piece of starfish to eat.

The starfish will grow a new arm to replace its lost one.

Sundial shell

This mollusk shell is neatly coiled into a round, flattish spiral. As the coils of the shell grow, they leave a hollow up the center, like a winding spiral staircase. Sundial shells live on tropical sandy shores.

The map cowrie has a pattern like a branching road or river on its shell.

The narrow shell opening has rows of teeth on either side.

Top of shell

Bottom of shell

Colorful cowries

You can recognize cowries by their oval shape and smooth, glossy shell. The shell opening is a long narrow slit and out of here the mantle of the living snail spreads across the shell.

Ribs look like strings of a harp.

Big foot

The harp shell snail can burrow or glide across the sand on its enormous foot. Its foot has another use, too – if grabbed by a predator, the end breaks off and allows the snail to escape.

When alive, the cowrie's mantle spreads out over its shell.

Open ocean shells

Most shelly sea creatures live in shallow waters near the coast. But there are ones that you rarely see, far from land, in the deep waters of the open sea. Some mollusks float and drift near the surface of the ocean with jellyfish, prawns, and other creatures. Other mollusks, along with pale, spindly-legged crabs and lobsters, live in the murky depths at the bottom of the sea.

Bubble raft snail
This sea snail hangs upside down at the surface of the sea and keeps itself afloat by clinging to a raft made out of bubbles. It feeds on small jellyfish and other floating animals.

See-through shell
No bigger than your fingernail, this tiny carnivorous sea snail swims along upside down, using its broad, spreading foot like a fin. Its thin, transparent shell makes it almost invisible to hungry fish.

Spidery legs for crawling along seabed

Monster claws
The giant Japanese spider uses its enormous pincer claws to grab prey – the claws are longer than a tall adult!

The living nautilus can control the depth at which it floats. All it does is adjust the amount of air inside its shell.

Inside the spiral shell are many pearl-lined compartments. The animal lives in the biggest one.

Shelled octopus

The pearly nautilus is a bit like an octopus with a shell. More than 30 tentacles stick out from the shell and catch prey. It moves by jet propulsion, squirting water out through a funnel under its head.

Strong, paddlelike flippers for swimming and diving

Can you see the ridges on the shell? These help the leatherback to swim very fast.

Jellyfish eater

Instead of a shelly back, the leatherback turtle has a tough leathery skin. It is a powerful swimmer and wanders far out to sea. The leatherback eats mainly jellyfish – but it never gets stung!

Index

Leaping cockle

MNO

Whelk shell

PR

Sea urchin test

Starfish

Acknowledgments

**Dorling Kindersley
would like to thank:**
Frank Greenaway for
photography on pages 11, 12
14, 19, 20, 24, 30, 31, 37, 42,
53.

Susan Downing, Sharon
Grant, and Wilfrid Wood for
design assistance.
Michele Lynch for editorial
assistance and research.
Jane Parker for the index.
Sea Life Centre, Weymouth,
for supplying shells for
photography.

Illustrations by:
Julie Anderson, Sophie
Griller, Nick Hewetson,
Danny Pyne, Peter Visscher.